THE RETRONAUT GUIDE TO
KEEPING PETS

THE RETRONAUT GUIDE TO
KEEPING PETS

WOLFGANG WILD

ilex

An Hachette UK Company
www.hachette.co.uk

First published in the UK in 2016 by ILEX, a division of Octopus Publishing Group Ltd
Carmelite House, 50 Victoria Embankment, London, EC4Y 0DZ
www.octopusbooks.co.uk

Design, layout, and text copyright
© Octopus Publishing Group 2016

Distributed in the US by Hachette Book Group
1290 Avenue of the Americas, 4th and 5th Floors, New York, NY 10020

Distributed in Canada by Canadian Manda Group
664 Annete St., Toronto, Ontario, Canada M6S 2C8

Publisher: **Roly Allen**
Commissioning Editor: **Zara Larcombe**
Managing Specialist Editor: **Frank Gallaugher**
Senior Project Editor: **Natalia Price-Cabrera**
Editor: **Rachel Silverlight**
Art Director: **Julie Weir**
Designer: **Tina Smith**
Assistant Production Manager: **Lucy Carter**

ISBN 978-1-78157-299-3

A CIP catalogue record for this book is available from the British Library

Printed in China

CONTENTS

6   Introduction
8   A bit of an animal
10 Aping humans
12 As cats do
16 Astrocats
20 Audition
24 Bath time
26 Bizarre
28 Board games
30 Camera

32 Cat predicaments
34 Childcare
36 Chilly
38 Cliché
40 Cuddles
42 Dinner time
44 Domesticated
46 Don't try this at home
50 Down on the farm

52 Easy rider
54 Facial
56 Fashion
58 For want of a horse
60 Get stuffed
64 Got the bird
68 In motion
72 In the pub
74 In the wars
76 Keep it unreal
78 Life with the lions
82 Masks
84 Mechanical elephant
86 Milking
88 Music tames the savage beast
92 Pipe smokers
94 Play the game
96 Politicians
98 Rabbit rabbit
100 Readers
102 Ride in style
104 Salon
106 Sea lions / seals
108 Spider!
110 Teatime
112 Technology
114 Transport
118 TV
120 Under my umbrella
122 Washday
124 What? and cart
126 You hum it and I'll play it
128 Acknowledgments / Picture credits

INTRODUCTION

Retronaut—the past like you wouldn't believe—is all about tearing little holes in your map of time. Here's how it works. You and I are walking around in the world, each with a map of the past in our heads. Our maps have been assembled from the sum total of every picture, every film, every sound, every song and every story of the past that we have encountered across our lives. Our minds stitch all these pieces together into our mental maps of time, and we each call our own map "the past."

Your map and my map are different—we each have memories that the other doesn't. And events that loom large on my map may not feature on yours at all—and vice versa. Some events, though, are obvious features on both our maps—like the Millennium, 9/11, and the two World Wars. But here's the thing. They are foggy, blurred, indistinct. Some parts of our maps are very detailed indeed, others have almost no detail at all. We use single words to sum up entire decades—the "Swinging" Sixties, the "Roaring" Twenties. And, by and large, our maps are in black and white. Because so many of the photographs we have seen of the past are black and white, even though logically we know the past was full of color, our maps are mainly in monochrome. Not only that, the people on our maps are walking very fast, just as they do in early films. And the people are either silent, or they speak in tiny, tinny voices.

The result is that when we imagine the past, it's often as something sepia, stiff, dusty—and

dead. And that's where Retronaut comes in. Retronaut knows that "the past" as something different from the present, different from this moment, from "now"—this past—does not exist. The past was, and is, all part of a very long "now." There is no division between "now" and "then." And no one has ever lived in "the past"—they have only ever lived in "now," but it was a different version. And so, Retronaut is dedicated to hunting down pictures, film, sound, stories and songs that don't feature on our maps. That do not seem like the past at all. That tear tiny holes in our mental maps of time. We want to show that, in the words of William Faulkner: "the past is never dead. It is not even past."

Retronaut came about because ever since I was a child, I have wanted to do one thing—go back in time. As a boy, I was fascinated by the wonder of the past. It seemed to me to be as exotic as another country—but one I could never visit. That seemed to me to be a shame, to say the least. Almost a design flaw in the universe. And so I fell in love with children's stories of time-travel, of people who

NO ONE HAS EVER LIVED IN "THE PAST" —THEY HAVE ONLY EVER LIVED IN "NOW," BUT IT WAS A DIFFERENT VERSION.

discovered a secret door that led them back into times gone. I looked and looked for my secret door, but never found it. Wanting to go back in time is not an obvious career choice, and so I buried my desire for years, decades, until it was reawakened when I discovered a book of color photographs from the 1940s. These color pictures were of the past, but they didn't look like the past at all—they were not sepia, stiff, dusty or dead. They looked just like "now." The color dissolved away the distance, like polish dissolving tarnish on a ring.

These old color photographs were my door. For the next few years, walking through my door became my passion. I avidly collected as many color pictures of the past as I could, finding them in second-hand book shops and charity shops—though rarely online. Soon, I found other doors as well as early color photography. I realised that all I had to look out for was something—anything—that didn't fit with the way I imagined the past, that didn't belong on my mental map. Find that, and I would have given myself a time-travel hit. This is how I got that hit. For a moment, I would do a mental double-take. My head would be temporally dislocated. "That can't be from the year it says it's from!" I would think. "What's happened? Either I have traveled in time, or the way I imagine that year is wrong." Then there would be a pause, and then I would have to change the way I imagined that point in time. The material had made a hole in my map of the past.

For many years, I collected all the

photographs I found—and the sounds, and the videos, and the illustrations—on my Mac. Then, one day in the Autumn of 2009, I met a friend of mine, John, in a Lebanese cafe in Paddington, London. I was showing John the collection on my computer. "You should start a blog," he said…Knowing nothing about blogging, I googled "What to call your blog." It seemed that "How to…" was a good start—how to bath your dog, how to make your lawn greener etc. Well, I wanted to show people how they could go back in time—or at least feel like they had, even just for a nano-second. But "How to go back in time" didn't seem quite cool enough. What was a word for someone who went back? Like an astronaut, but only going backwards? A "retronaut."

And so I started my shiny new blog at the beginning of January 2010. I loved creating it, and adding to it. It also gave me a chance to do something that I had always wanted to do, but never had the opportunity to do before—to curate. I am not a trained curator, nor ever likely to be, and a professional curator is a highly specialized job. But to be able to choose, show, and share pictures in the way I wanted to was deeply satisfying. In a very small way, I was a curator. For three weeks the audience for Retronaut was approximately two—my mother and I. And between us we amassed around 200 hits a day. Then, one day, at the end of January, one of the posts went viral, and ended up on the front page of *Reddit*. The post was a set of color high-resolution Kodachrome pictures of central London in 1949, taken by

THIS BOOK IS CRAMMED WITH PHOTOGRAPHS OF ANIMALS OF THE PAST LIKE YOU WOULDN'T BELIEVE.

the beautifully named Chalmers Butterfield. People would look at these gorgeous, super-colorful, super-resolution shots. "Cool pictures," they would say. "Is that a film-set? It can't be, it's too real. But it looks like a digital picture—and it's in color. I didn't think they even had color in 1949!" And then their mind would do the double-take, the hole in their map of the past was torn. And then they would share the pictures with their friends.

The result for me was 30,000 hits in one day. And the rest is history. Or rather, Retronaut. The underlying message of Retronaut is that what may seem to us today to be fixed, essential, and inevitable, may simply be another version of now. It's a message of freedom and potential. Nothing is fixed, everything can be changed, remixed, recurated. And that includes ourselves.

For this book, we have chosen to focus on the subject of pets. As well as the fact that the internet is largely dominated by animals—and primarily by kittens—it is also probable that a large number of us have at one time or another shared a home with an

animal or two. But just over a hundred years ago, there was no doubt about it. Animals were an essential and unavoidably obvious part of daily life for almost all of our society. Step out onto the street in the early years of the twentieth century, and you would see a horse—or at least the evidence that one had passed by very recently. That's no longer the case for most of us. But it's not the only way in which the place of animals in our world has changed across the last century or so. This book is crammed with photographs of animals of the past like you wouldn't believe. Improbable and impossible pets. Animals in every form of fancy-dress, and non-fancy-dress. Animals helping in the home. Animals making themselves at home. Animals making war. Animals making peace. Animals in the road. Animals on the road. Animals using technology. Technology using animals. Animals creating art. Animals creating chaos. Famous animals. Infamous animals. Animals showing off. And animals showing us up. Big time.

The thread that ties each of these photographs together is that we at Retronaut think they are very unlikely to already be on your map of the past. We think they are going to take your map and tear tiny holes in it. Together, they represent a slice of the animal kingdom that is still hard to believe. A different animal past. And that is what Retronaut is all about.

Wolfgang Wild, author

1946: Publicist Jim Moran reads Betty MacDonald's book *The Egg and I* to a gathering of ostriches. Location not known.

1958: 17-year-old Bianca Passarge of Hamburg dresses up as a cat, complete with furry tail, and dances on wine bottles. Her performance was based on a dream and she practiced for eight hours every day in order to perfect her dance.

1955: An orang-utan expresses itself through the medium of paint. Location not known.

RIGHT **1930:** George, the chimpanzee at London's Kids Zoo, attempts to capture a portrait of Larry the Lamb.

1943: Photographer Gjon Mili's cat Blackie nibbling the foot of a young acrobat.

1958: The traditional cat–mouse conflict is thrown into reverse gear.

1925: Mother cat Blackie halts traffic as she transports her five kittens, one by one, across Lafayette St. in lower Manhattan, USA. Police Office James Cudmore gives a helping hand.

1941: A cat is rescued after an air-raid bomb crashed through the roof of a shelter in London during World War 1.

LEFT, RIGHT, AND
OVERLEAF **1968:**
A cat is dropped
upside down to
demonstrate how
a cat's movements
while falling can
be imitated by
astronauts in space.
The experiment—
designed to explore
the nature of
moving in zero-
gravity—substituted
a trampolinist in
a space suit for
an astronaut.

1951: MGM associate producer Sidney Franklin Jr. gives Hollywood lion, Fearless Fagan, a voice test.

RIGHT **1934:** Walt Disney trying to coax a penguin into performing for the camera, for a "Silly Symphony" entitled "Peculiar Penguins."

1961: Owners with their black cats, waiting in line to be auditioned for the movie *Tales of Terror.*

RIGHT **1947:** Radio sound effects man, Don Bain, working Emily Alyce the poodle and Kitty the cat into a frenzy on the radio.

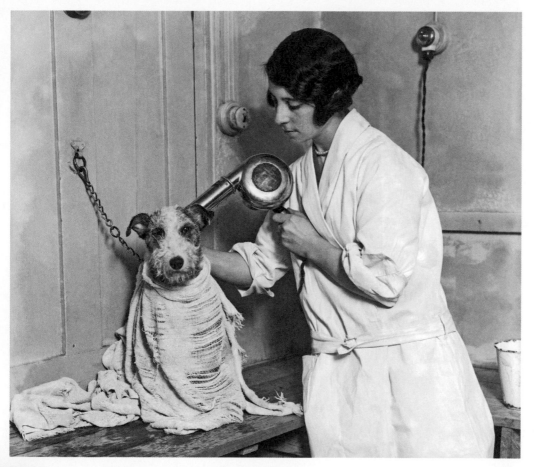

1930: A dog has
a bath and blow
dry at a parlour in
Kensington, London.

c. 1950s: Boris the Afghan has his bath in the family bathroom. Location not known.

1960: A praying mantis playing a miniature piano. Location not known.

RIGHT **1970:** In California, USA, a 40-year-old Koi carp has learned to feed from a baby's bottle.

LEFT **1933:** A lamb and a cat enjoying a game of draughts, watched over by a bantam hen, in Somerset, England.

1955: A young girl watches Fifi the chimpanzee contemplate her next move in a game of chess at London Zoo.

1860: The rear-view of a canine amateur photographer.

RIGHT **1958:** Two kittens debate photographic techniques.

1955: A pair of kittens parachute to earth for reasons that are not clear. Location not known.

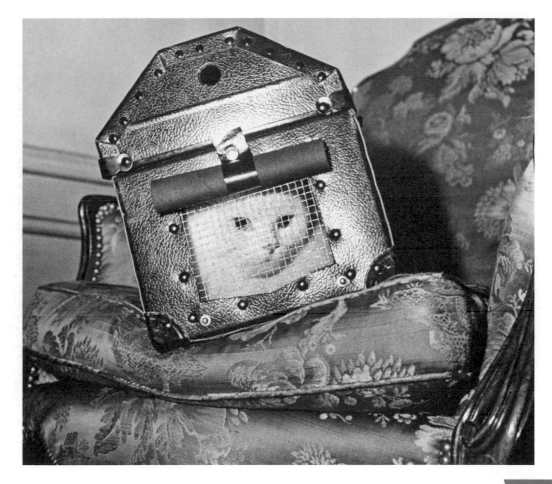

1941: A cat in a bombproof carrier during a World War II air raid.

1955: Blondie, the pet lion, looks pleased as her owner Charles Hipp places his baby granddaughter Karen on Blondie's back.

LEFT **c. 1930s:** In Los Angeles, California, three-year-old Betty Bench shares a meal with her dolls and Nubia the lion cub.

1950: A turkey wrapped up in a blanket and scarf to keep it warm and free from colds and chills, Hertfordshire, England.

c. 1950: In a studio, a giraffe has its neck insulated. Location not known.

LEFT **1938:** Comet, an elephant from Chessington Zoo, spends the weekend working as a waiter at the Trocadero Restaurant in London's busy Piccadilly Circus.

1950: In a china shop in Malvern, England—a bull.

1948: A Miss Davis from Chertsey, England, embraces her pet alligator.

RIGHT **1908:** A young crocodile is the perfect new pet for ladies, as demonstrated by this woman and her dog at Bostock's Jungle, Earls Court in London.

LEFT **1984:** A butler serves a meal to a table of dogs in an upmarket Knightsbridge restaurant, London.

1940: A kitten emerges from a bowl of milk. Location not known.

1954: An Alsatian dog balancing four cups and saucers on its head. Location not known.

RIGHT **1936:** Wall of Death rider "Tornado" Smith and his wife having tea with their pet lion and lamb.

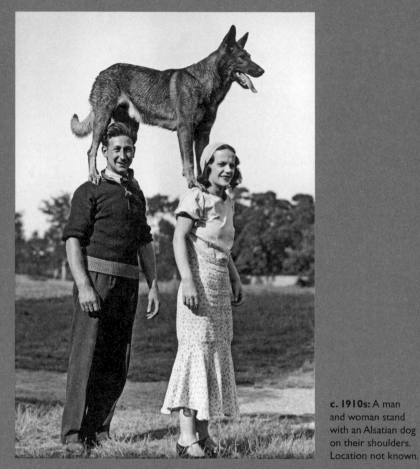

c. 1910s: A man and woman stand with an Alsatian dog on their shoulders. Location not known.

1938: An elephant's foot covers a man's face. Location not known.

1933: Animal tamer Marjorie Kemp with her favorite lion, Sultan, in a Wall of Death fairground ride.

1957: A bear cub hitches a ride on a little boy's back. Location not known.

LEFT **c. 1913:**
Madame de L'Oris
of the Busch circus
with her trained
cows. Location not
known.

1947: A man lays
on one of his
trained cows.
Location not known.

1905: On Independence Day, Eunice Padfield and her horse thrill the holiday crowds as they plunge from a high platform into a pool of water below, in Colorado, USA.

RIGHT **1959:** A horse-back cat takes an obstacle in its stride. Location not known.

1954: Breeder Carl A. Anderson displays a group of monarch butterflies.

c. 1930s: A
beekeeper wearing
a unique beard of
200,000 bees.

1960: A model sports a shawl with a photographic rendition of a terrier dog—and the terrier sits beside her.

1958: At the League of Women Voters Convention, a woman wears a crab hat.

LEFT 1935: A motorist pauses as Laffin Leslie, an 18-year-old dwarf, guides Jimmy, the "only rideable zebra in the world," across a road in Berkshire, England.

c. 1915: A zebra and trap, and a tram vie for business in Brixton, London.

1986: A taxidermist
in Denver, Colorado,
USA, decorates a
polar bear for the
holiday season.

1964: A 2,000-pound stuffed crocodile, shot by the former governor of New Mexico while on safari in Africa.

1962: An assistant at Charles Gerrard's London taxidermy workshop brings out a stuffed leopard for the customer.

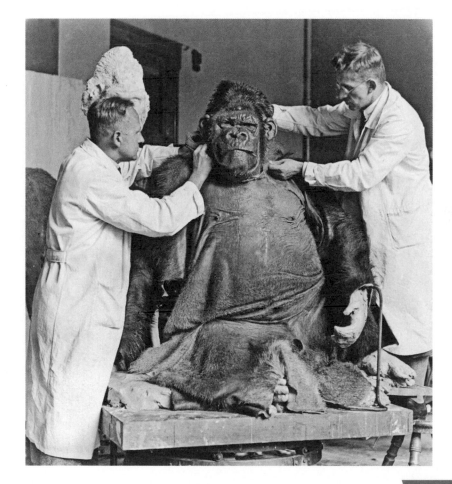

1936: Bobby the gorilla, darling of the Berliner zoo, is reshaped after his death.

1937: Mrs Lockyer from Stoke-on-Trent, England, takes her pet goose out on a shopping trip.

RIGHT **1948:** An owl acts as a spindle for a woman's wool. Location not known.

1936: A bemused man watches two swans who make regular visits to a social club to warm themselves by the fire. Location not known.

RIGHT **1936:** Billy the pet goose has a cup of tea with his mistress. Location not known.

LEFT **1938:** A show-jumper launches his horse over a bed in Colchester, England.

1935: A Texas longhorn steer leaps over a car at the 4th Annual Santa Monica Rodeo, USA.

c. 1950: A cat demonstrates its predatory skills as it attempts to pluck a fish from the air. Location not known.

1961: Montezuma, the tree ocelot, leaps from the door of the Manhattan apartment where it is kept as a pet.

LOAFERS BAR

c. 1975: 10-year-old Maureen the elephant enters the Loafers Bar of the Cottage Loaf Pub.

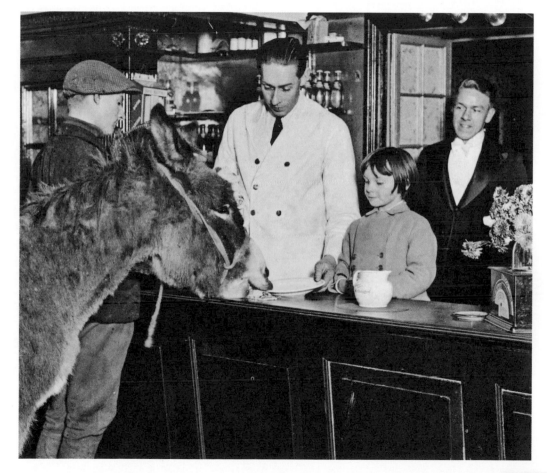

1934: The Ship Inn, Alveston, England is visited by a donkey that grazes in the adjoining field.

LEFT **1939:** Three Airedale dogs wearing gas masks at a kennel in Surrey, England.

1915: During World War I a dog is dressed up as a German soldier. Location not known.

1925: A full-size model elephant atop a promotional car. Location not known.

RIGHT **1937:** Two men dressed as a zebra step out of a London taxi on their way to a circus performance.

1971: American actress Melanie Griffith jumps into a swimming pool at her home in California as her family's pet lion, Neil, grabs and goes to bite her leg,

RIGHT 1971: American actress and animal activist Tippi Hedren reads a newspaper as she leans against Neil.

1971: Melanie
Griffith in the family
swimming pool
with Neil.

1971: Tippi Hedren and Neil explore the fridge.

1948: Pablo Picasso poses in a large bull head mask and a pair of swimming trunks on a French beach.

1933: Sandwichmen being made up in their headgear at the Agricultural Hall, London.

1948: A circus elephant displays a board stating "FOR SALE OR FOR LEASE" during a rehearsal for the Ringling Bros. and Barnum & Bailey Circus, Sarasota, Florida, USA.

1950: A boy plays with the trunk of a full-sized mechanical elephant while his friends enjoy a ride on its back in Essex, England.

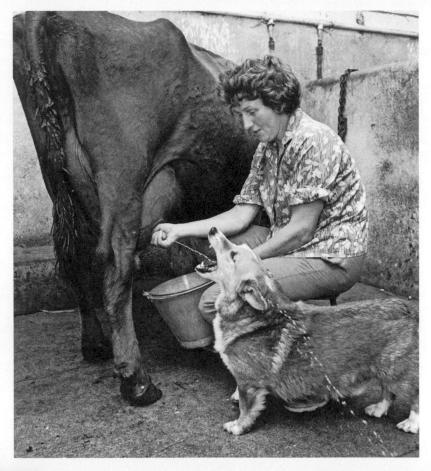

1963: Animal lover Olive Tate directing milk into her corgi dog Buster's mouth while milking a cow.

RIGHT **1940:** The Actress Dorothy Henry milks a cow on stage, Philadelphia, USA.

LEFT **1930:** A man plays the flute accompanied by a tame bird and red squirrel. Location not known.

1926: Mr Macfrisco, the singing sea lion, has a singing lesson. Location not known.

1929: A canine actor is unimpressed by the musical efforts of her mistress. Location not known.

1909: A zookeeper serenades a bear with a gramophone. Location not known.

1984: Zillah the pipe-smoking bull mastiff. Location not known.

1924: Jiggs, the pet fire dog of the Hollywood Fire Department, is ready at the wheel.

1963: American horse and comic actor Bamboo Harvester aka "Mr Ed" swings at a pitch.

RIGHT **1936:** Two elephants playing cricket on the beach at Skegness, England.

1938: Nazi leader Hermann Goering plays with one of his pet lion cubs. Location not known.

1924: Italian Fascist Dictator Benito Mussolini going for a drive with Ras, his pet lion cub. Location not known.

LEFT **c. 1930:** A pair of stuffed rabbits in aprons carry a basket of eggs between them. Location not known.

1928: Actress Patricia Avery playing "shadow puppets" on the wall with a very large rabbit. Location not known.

1949: Four-year-old Carl Detroy looking through a picture-book with Marquis, one of his family's pet chimpanzees, at their home in Essex in England.

RIGHT **1928:** King penguins prepare to welcome the Prince of Wales to London Zoo for its centenary.

WELCOME
TO THE
PRINCE

1960s: West Berlin police dogs, Wolf and Hector, rehearse in their remote control car for the annual West Berlin police show at the Olympic Stadium.

RIGHT **1920:** An unusual way to transport a dog, Paris, France.

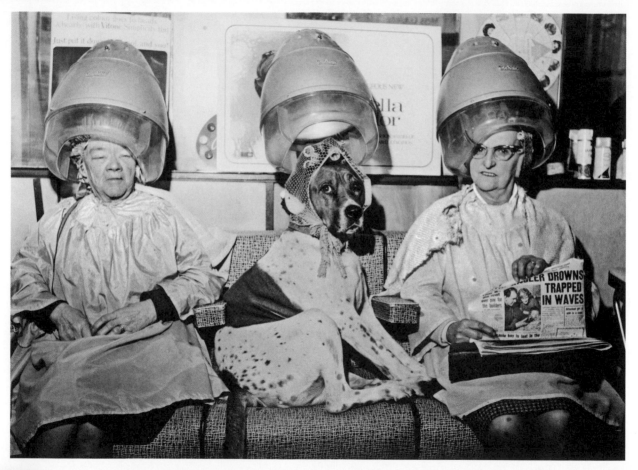

LEFT **1968:** A dog with its fur set in curlers at a London hairdressing salon.

1920s: At Marion's Beauty School in New York City, Miss Agnes O'Laughlin receives her treatment as does Bubble, her poodle.

1931: Two women in bathing suits share a snack with a couple of sea lions during a display held in Paris.

RIGHT **1932:** A young girl feeding an elephant seal at London Zoo.

1963: Beatles George Harrison, John Lennon, and Paul McCartney stare at a plastic spider perched on Ringo Starr's nose, backstage after their Sunday Night at the London Palladium show.

1948: Singer Jarmila Novotna wears a prize-winning headdress including bugs pasted on her shoulder.

LEFT **1949:** Farmer Mrs Maud Lee, her daughter Pat, and their pet lamb Betty, enjoy tea at their farmhouse, near Bristol, England.

1934: A dog dressed for a tea party. Location not known.

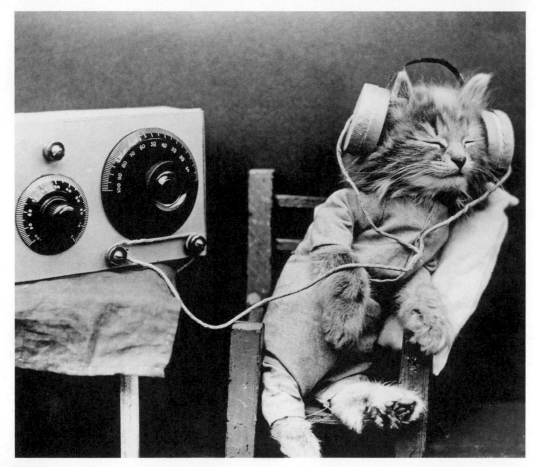

1926: A cat shuts out the rest of the world whilst listening to the radio. Location not known.

RIGHT **1927:** In Germany, dairy cows are serenaded during milking time, resulting in ten percent more milk yield.

c. 1960: A cow catches a ride on a Paris bus.

RIGHT **1951:** MGM producer Sidney Franklin Jr. chauffeurs Hollywood lion Fearless Fagan, his newly discovered star.

1963: Captain J. Edwards puts a seat belt on one of his alligators in the back seat of his car. Location not known.

1970: Five West HIghland terriers arriving at London's Crufts Dog Show in their traveling kennels balanced in a pram.

1934: Dogs watching one of their own on TV. Location not known.

RIGHT **1960s:** Cows watch TV on a farm in Devon, England.

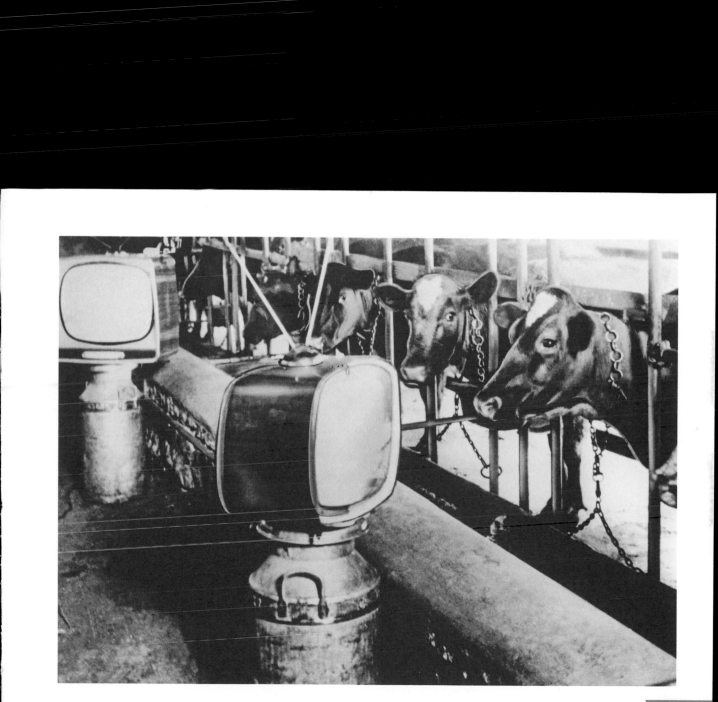

1989: Andy the goose was born without feet. Here he wears specially designed sneakers and rides a miniature bicycle complete with umbrella.

RIGHT **1928:** A horse takes shelter under an umbrella during a snowfall in Paris, France.

LEFT **1933:** A cat hangs out a row of tame and freshly washed rats on the washing line to dry.

1950s: A mother cocker spaniel attends to four puppies hanging in socks on a laundry clothesline. Location not known.

1935: A child in a wicker chariot drawn by a Saint Bernard dog. Location not known.

1930: A speeding ostrich carriage is stopped by the Los Angeles police.

1955: Kiba, a South American Puma, plays the piano. Location not known.

1921: A circus horse blows a brass instrument. Location not known.

PICTURE CREDITS

2 GraphicaArtis/Getty Images; 5 Getty Images/H. Armstrong Roberts/Retrofile; 8 Getty Images/George Strock/The LIFE Images Collection; 9 Getty Images/Carlo Polito/BIPs; 10 Getty Images/Hulton Archive; 11 Getty Images/Imagno; 12 Getty Images/Gjon Mili/The LIFE Picture Collection; 13 Corbis Bettmann; 14 Getty Images/Harry Warnecke/NY Daily News Archive via Getty Images; 15 Getty Images/Planet News Archive/SSPL; 16 Getty Images/Ralph Crane/The LIFE Picture Collection; 17 Getty Images/Ralph Crane/The LIFE Picture Collection; 18 Getty Images/Ralph Crane/The LIFE Picture Collection; 19 Getty Images/Ralph Crane/The LIFE Picture Collection; 20 Getty Images/Loomis Dean/The LIFE Premium Collection; 21 Getty Images/Hulton Archive; 22 Getty Images/Ralph Crane/The LIFE Picture Collection; 23 Getty Images/Lisa Larsen/The LIFE Images Collection; 24 Getty Images/SSPL; 25 Getty Images/Central Press; 26 Getty Images/Wendel; 27 Getty Images/Marti Coale/BIPs; 28 Getty Images/Fox Photos; 29 Getty Images/William Vanderson/Fox Photos; 30 Getty Images/London Stereoscopic Company; 31 Getty Images/Keystone-France/Gamma-Keystone via Getty Images; 32 Getty Images/Pearl Hall/Three Lions; 33 Getty Images/John Phillips/The LIFE Picture Collection; 34 Getty Images/Gamma-Keystone via Getty Images; 35 Getty Images/Joseph Scherschel/The LIFE Picture Collection; 36 Getty Images/Reg Speller/Fox Photos; 37 Getty Images/Keystone-France/Gamma-Keystone via Getty Images; 38 Getty Images/Fox Photos; 39 Getty Images/Popperfoto; 40 Getty Images/Charles Hewitt; 41 Getty Images/Topical Press Agency; 42 Getty Images/Nina Leen/The LIFE Picture Collection; 43 Getty Images/BIPs; 44 Getty Images/Keystone; 45 Getty Images/Fox Photos; 46 Getty Images/SSPL; 47 Getty Images/Heinrich Hoffmann/ullstein bild via Getty Images; 48 Getty Images/Imagno; 49 Getty Images/Nat Farbman/The LIFE Picture Collection; 50 Getty Images/Conrad Huenich/ullstein bild via Getty Images; 51 Getty Images/Nina Leen/The LIFE Picture Collection; 52 Getty Images/Underwood Archives; 53 Getty Images/ullstein bild/ullstein bild via Getty Images; 54 Getty Images/John Dominis/The LIFE Picture Collection; 55 Getty Images/Keystone; 56 Getty Images/Nina Leen/The LIFE Picture Collection; 57 Getty Images/Robert W. Kelley/The LIFE Picture Collection; 58 Getty Images/Jim Richardson/The Denver Post via Getty Images; 59 Getty Images/Ed Maker/The Denver Post via Getty Image; 60 Getty Images/Chris Ware/Keystone Features; 61 Getty Images/Dorothea von der Osten/ullstein bild via Getty Images; 62 Getty Images/Fox Photos; 63 Getty Images/Keystone; 64 Getty Images/Fox Photos; 65 Getty Images/Fox Photos; 66 Getty Images/Keystone-France/Gamma-Keystone via Getty Images; 67 Getty Images/FPG/Hulton Archive; 68 Getty Images/Popperfoto; 69 Getty Images/Al Fenn/The LIFE Picture Collection; 70 Corbis/Hulton-Deutsch Collection; 71 Getty Images/Fox Photos; 72 Getty Images/Keystone; 73 Corbis/adoc-photos; 74 Getty Images/Sean Sexton; 75 Getty Images/Reg Speller/Fox Photos; 76 Getty Images/Michael Rougier/The LIFE Picture Collection; 77 Getty Images/Michael Rougier/The LIFE Picture Collection; 78 Getty Images/Michael Rougier/The LIFE Picture Collection; 79 Getty Images/Michael Rougier/The LIFE Picture Collection; 80 Getty Images/Gjon Mili/Time & Life Pictures, © Succession Piccaso/DACS, London 2016; 81 Getty Images/Fox Photos; 82 Getty Images/Nina Leen; 83 Getty Images/Harold Clements/Express; 84 Getty Images/Keystone-France/Gamma-Keystone via Getty Images; 85 Getty Images/John Drysdale/Keystone Features; 86 Getty Images/ullstein bild/ullstein bild via Getty Images; 87 Getty Images/Topical Press Agency; 88 Getty Images/Margaret Chute; 89 Getty Images/Philipp Kester/ullstein bild via Getty Images; 90 Getty Images/SSPL; 91 Corbis/Bettmann; 92 Getty Images/CBS Photo Archive; 93 Getty Images/Reg Speller/Fox Photos; 94 Getty Images/PhotoQuest; 95 Getty Images/Keystone; 96 Getty Images/FPG; 97 Getty Images/Hulton Archive; 98 Getty Images/Charles Hewitt/Picture Post/Hulton Archive; 99 Getty Images/Keystone-France/Gamma-Keystone via Getty Images; 100 Corbis/Bettmann; 101 Getty Images/Gamma-Keystone via Getty Images; 102 Getty Images/Paul Fievez/BIPS/Hulton Archive; 103 Corbis/AS400 DB; 104 Getty Images/Fox Photos; 105 Corbis/FLPA/David Hosking; 106 Getty Images/Peter Hall/Keystone; 107 Getty Images/Bob Landry/The LIFE Images Collection; 108 Getty Images/Burchell/Fox Photos; 109 Getty Images/Fox Photos; 110 Getty Images/Monty Fresco/Topical Press Agency; 111 Getty Images/Underwood Archives; 112 Getty Images/Fox Photos; 113 Getty Images/Topical Press Agency; 114 Getty Images/Keystone/Hulton Archive; 115 Getty Images/Loomis Dean/The LIFE Premium Collection; 116 Getty Images/Keystone; 117 Getty Images/Keystone; 118 Getty Images/ullstein bild/ullstein bild via Getty Images; 119 Getty Images/Keystone-France/Gamma-Keystone via Getty Images; 120 Getty Images/Keith Philpott/The LIFE Images Collection; 121 Getty Images/Gamma-Keystone via Getty Images; 122 Getty Images/Central Press; 123 Corbis/ClassicStock; 124 Getty Images/Imagno; 125 Getty Images/Imagno; 126 Getty Images/Sherman/Three Lions; 127 Getty Images/Hulton Archive; 128 Getty Images/Reinhold Thiele/Topical Press Agency.

ACKNOWLEDGMENTS

Thank you to Zara Larcombe, Natalia Price-Cabrera, Tina Smith, Roly Allen, and Andrew Gordon. Thank you also to Alex Q. Arbuckle, Stephanie Buck, Pete Cashmore, Dustin Drankoski, Mike Kriak, Adam Ostrow, Chris Phillips, Jim Roberts, Christoph Shcholz, and Darren Tome. Special thanks to digital curator Amanda Uren.